FRENCH SEASIDE STYLE

FRENCH SEASIDE STYLE

Text and photographs by Sébastien Siraudeau

Flammarion

Contents

Introduction

French Seaside Style. It's an invitation to bring your travel memories home, infusing it with light and serenity. France is a country of two coastlines, caught between the tantalizing embrace of the ocean—the stormy Atlantic seaboard with its towering cliffs, windswept beaches, and pounding surf—and the sea, the tideless, azure calm of the Mediterranean, basking in the southern sun beyond the terra-cotta rooftiles and green-black umbrella pines of the Côte d'Azur. Those diverse sundrenched waters bring travelers back year after year to their favorite seaside retreat: a granite *longère* on the coast of Brittany, a time-honored hotel on the Bassin d'Arcachon, a Provençal hideaway so near, yet so far, from the madding crowds of Saint-Tropez, an island cottage buffeted by the wind and waves.

France has its share of adventurers and mariners, explorers and shipwrecked sailors: romantic images of the sea fueled by the rapturous visions of poets and painters alike. But for many, the sea is a way of life—from the ship's captains of yore, returning home to the Breton seaports, to today's Finistère fishermen, or championship yacht crews training at La Trinité. For many more, the sea is a source of smaller pleasures—childhood holidays, sandcastles, collecting mussels and whelks for supper. Memories to treasure— in collections of scallop shells or driftwood, starfish, or oddly shaped pebbles picked up in quiet creeks along coastal footpaths (the old *sentiers des douaniers,* once used by customs officials in hot pursuit of smugglers).

The essence of the sea is captured in a jar piled high with gleaming shards of mother-of-pearl, a cloche protecting the fragile tracery of a dried sea fan, or a ship-in-a-bottle. Once displayed in the corner of a room, these objects can fill an entire house with their maritime aura.

The colors of the sea too—pale sky blue or soft gray, bright white, vibrant primaries or delicate washes, accent walls and furniture painted and repainted like the hull of a boat. Whoever visits the sea feels the urge to bring it home—every interior is an island, a snug cabin, a much-loved ship ready to set sail on the high seas of the imagination.

Coast to Coast

From the Channel to the Mediterranean, France's myriad seascapes inspire homes and interiors to match.

A converted boatshed

Sophie and Patrick Deloison
LE LOFT
Vacation apartment
1 quai du Romerel, 80230 Saint-Valery-sur-Somme
www.picardieweb.com/deloison
+ 33 (0)3 22 26 92 17

A shaft of sunlight strikes the Eiffel Tower, and every Parisian's fancy turns to thoughts of escape. The sweeping waterscapes of the Somme estuary are the French capital's nearest (seaside) port of call: the beach at Crotoy, Marquenterre nature reserve, the harbor at Saint-Valery. Picardy's corner of seaside heaven is well-loved for its cobbled quaysides, authentic charm, and fabulous seafood market. The region's brick-and-timber fishermen's cottages are in high demand, and every metropolitan weekender dreams of finding a small, well-equipped hideaway for a breath of sea air. Would a stylish loft be too much to ask? Sophie and Patrick Deloison have created just that, in an old boatshed converted with flair and skill by Patrick himself, a beachcombing handyman and professional antiques dealer. The tall building is divided into two levels. The ground floor is a working antiques warehouse, while the loft occupies the "cathedral" mezzanine above— a wooden structure built by a ship's carpenter and decorated in imaginative, theatrical style, using found objects and cleverly recycled pieces put to new uses. The essence of seaside charm.

Scrubbed driftwood, bare brick, heavy wooden
floorboards, natural linen. Hanging like fishermen's
ex-votos from the rafters, a flotilla of miniature
canoes, junks, and other assorted craft.
The Robinson Crusoe interior is flooded with natural
light from ten glass doors ranged along one wall,
like a Parisian artist's studio.

A curious buffalo-head trophy above a painting
by Robert Hanès (a long-time resident
of Saint-Valery). Separating the bedroom
from the bathroom, an open-work balustrade
from a *café-dancing* in a nearby village.

For family getaways

Marina and Christophe Ducharme
LE SÉNÉCHAL
Hotel and guesthouses
6 rue Gambetta, 17590 Ars-en-Ré
www.hotel-le-senechal.com
+33 (0)5 46 29 40 42

Ten years. A landmark anniversary for Marina and Christophe Ducharme and their small hotel on the Île de Ré, a tiny island connected to the town of La Rochelle since 1988 by the graceful arc of a two-mile bridge. To begin at the beginning: the Ducharmes were married here, and acquired the hotel almost by accident. After experiencing at first hand the difficulties of taking three small children on a hotel vacation, they decided to create their own perfect place for short family breaks. Christophe—a professional architect—took charge of converting the rambling collection of buildings, using every last scrap of space to create a friendly, welcoming home-from-home. With rooms of all sizes and prices, Le Sénéchal quickly attracted an eclectic, enthusiastic clientele. One summer season led to another, bringing new plans and projects. First, extra bedrooms were created in the old Post Office building next door, connected to the hotel by a series of intimate patios and tiny courtyard gardens. Next came a loft, a series of cottages—first one, then two, now four. What will be next?

Beneath a string of firefly lights, the loft typifies the hotel's chic, informal style, with a mix of fine and rustic materials. Old stone, bare brick, and a partition wall of untreated pine along the whole length of the room (concealing the bathroom and WC) create an elegant setting for quality bric-a-brac furniture finds, painted black.

Natural materials and fine patinas

The island's clear Atlantic light suffuses the charming warren of buildings and rooms,
connected by their original doorways, partially glass-paned partition walls.
Each room is a unique expression of the hotel's distinctive style, and its owners' love of simple,
natural materials and objects.

Small stools, church benches, bistro chairs, bamboo garden tables, and a host
of other modest pieces were picked up at bric-a-brac sales in the village, scrubbed bare
or repatinated. Blending perfectly with their setting, each piece embodies the hotel's essential
blend of traditional and contemporary style: unpretentious, simple and full
of charm, like a much-loved vacation home.

Down on the beach

France Ladouceur
LE CHÂTEAU DE SABLE
Guesthouse
Avenue des Anthémis, 83240 Cavalaire-sur-Mer
www.chateaudesable.net
+ 33 (0)4 94 00 45 90

France Ladouceur freely admits that life in Cavalaire-sur-Mer is an endless vacation. Her beachfront house is the last word in stylish living-on-sea. Anchored at the far end of Cavalaire beach, Le Château de Sable—transformed from the solid foundations of a 1960's villa—is one sandcastle that's here to stay. In a fairytale setting, it is a child's dream house for carefree vacations. With the help of her two daughters, France has created a timeless, effortlessly elegant setting, a bastion of serene calm. Bedrooms gaze out to sea from private balconies, and the hotel's drawing room extends into the garden, with huge tables and solid wooden benches lounging quietly beneath the umbrella pines. A path of stepping stones dots the grass, leading to a small gate that opens directly onto the beach, its carpet of white sand an open invitation to your morning dip. Or candlelit dinners of fine Provençal cuisine, served overlooking the sea in summer.

Canoe paddles, a model boat, a fisherman's stool, a panama hat, and a straw boater,
reminding us that the sea is just around the corner. The stylish interior is a mix
of flea-market finds and new pieces crafted from recycled materials, like the large
dining-room table, made from broad wooden planks placed on trestles.

The decor is a haven of rustic charm, with essential modern comforts. The finest natural, local materials blend with the gentle color scheme: a subtle harmony of vintage linen, cotton or blended textiles, distressed wood, whitewash, rich polished leather, and ethereal ironwork. For rainy days (they are few) a padded club armchair or a *méridienne* covered in chocolate-colored linen stand waiting indoors.

By the light of the sea

Where the mountains meet the sea

Constance Ladouceur
LA MAISON DE CONSTANCE
Guesthouse
Hameau du Dattier, 83240 Cavalaire-sur-Mer
+ 33 (0)4 94 00 45 90

Constance Ladouceur grew up at Le Château de Sable, her mother's beachside retreat at Cavalaire-sur-Mer. When she decided to create a holiday hideaway of her own, she turned to the last wild stretches of the Côte d'Azur, between Hyères and Saint-Tropez, to the hidden quiet of a region known only to a lucky few. From the extraordinary Mediterranean gardens at Rayol to the secluded village of Ramatuelle, a delightful coast path explores the unspoiled landscapes of the Massif des Maures. Far from the bustling seaside town of Cavalaire, a handful of scattered houses gaze out to sea, and the trio of islands known as the Îles d'Or. Hameau du Dattier is an isolated hamlet, a former stop on the route taken by the historic Train des Pignes. All that remains of the railway today is a long tunnel burrowing deep into the mountain. Constance created her delightful home by connecting two adjacent buildings, surrounded by a swimming pool, and pergolas, terraces, and balconies that were created to make the most of the panoramic views. Far below, Constance can catch a glimpse of her childhood beach, and dreams of other castles, waiting to be built.

The villa is an ideal retreat for large family
gatherings and holidays. The huge living room
and kitchen open onto the terrace,
with azure views of the distant Mediterranean.
Constance's decor draws on her collection
of naïf objects and bric-a-brac finds: a lobster trap,
vintage glass jars filled with dried petals,
soft furnishings in linen and hemp.

Burgundy stone floors and doors made from recycled vintage wood add to the authentic
atmosphere and charm of the house. On the upper floor, a large bedroom opens onto
a balcony reminiscent of the quirky, hand-built seaside chalets found scattered along
this part of the Mediterranean coast. The doors and furniture were all sourced at flea markets,
or specially made by Constance's friend Mathilde Labrouche, recreating the raw,
naturally worn patina of driftwood washed by the wind and salt water.

Harbor Views

In fishermen's cottages and seafaring
ports, the sea is seen and felt—
a constant presence, inspiring
voyages of the imagination.

Full sail

Martine and Éric Rousseau
KERELEVEN
Guesthouse
11 chemin de la Hune, 56470 La Trinité-sur-Mer
www.kereleven.com
+ 33 (0)2 97 55 75 07

Fine weather, calm seas. A flurry of wind, and Éric Rousseau can sit back and enjoy the majestic spectacle of some of the world's finest racing yachts from his terrace overlooking the celebrated *chenal*—the narrow arm of sea reaching inland from the Atlantic at La Trinité-sur-Mer, in southeastern Brittany. It's a perfect setting. When Éric decided to weigh anchor and devote himself to his first passion—maritime photography— he set a course for La Trinité, one of France's best-known seafaring towns, and a training base for top international yacht crews. Éric spent his vacations here, in a small fisherman's cottage owned by his parents—a traditional *penty* with pitched slate roofs, built in the time-honored way, at right angles to the sea. Extensive work was needed to "turn the house around" and maximize the sea views. Terraces were a priority—and now there are three. Next, the house was extended with the help of local artisans and friends—joiners, carpenters, and painters—each of whom now has a guest room named for him (or her) in the main part of the building. With a nod to the famous Gitana 11 yacht, the winner of the legendary Route du Rhum transatlantic race, Éric has named his house Kereleven: "house no. 11" in Breton.

Plum-colored walls and headboards made from old doors patinated with gold leaf
and sparse touches of bright yellow or red create a warm, cozy atmosphere
in this bedroom. Éric has brought together contemporary objects and family treasures,
like this antique Hotchkiss trunk, which belonged to the owner's grandfather.

The decor is inspired by cargo ships and sailing
yachts alike. One of Éric's ancestors
was the inventor of the Velox, a nineteenth-century
schooner. To the two-tone walls, extending the line
of the *chenal*'s horizon glimpsed from the window,
animated by the graceful ballet of passing yachts,
are attached old seascapes.

A rooftop perch

Jessica and Pako
AU VIEUX PANIER
Guesthouse
13 rue du Panier, 13002 Marseille
www.auvieuxpanier.com
+ 33 (0)4 91 91 23 72

Marseille, just as you imagined it always would be: its Old Port and narrow, winding streets climbing steeply from the waterfront to the heart of the neighborhood known as the Panier. Between the tall, tightly packed houses, children play, voices echo from behind half-closed shutters, and the sea is a thousand miles away. Looking up, you sense another life, beyond the rooftops. And the view? Just step through Jessica and Pako's front door (a former Corsican grocery store with its picturesque shop front and sign still intact). The young owners—keen travelers, with a strong interest in design and art—have remodeled the interior of this tall, narrow townhouse. After extensive rebuilding, and invitations to local artists to decorate the newly created space, the guesthouse finally opened its doors on the threshold of summer. The terra-cotta-tiled staircase serves the guest bedrooms, the owners' apartment, and finally the roof—the terrace of their dreams, with a stunning view of the city, its rooftops and balconies, the striped dome of Sainte-Marie-Majeure (*"la Major,"* the much-loved sentinel at the entrance to the Old Port). And the sea—the glorious Côte Bleue—on the horizon.

On the ground floor, the living room and dining room
combine to create a friendly communal space.
The minimalist black-and-white walls are offset
by a decorative mix of vintage, industrial, and Quaker
style. One section of wall is covered with a thick sheet
of metal, supporting a clever arrangement
of magnetized tablet shelves, an ampersand
from an old shop sign, and a changing display
of posters, papers, and pictures.

Whitelines, Balcon New-Yorkais: each guest room
is named for a different part of the world,
and decorated by a different artist. The *Travel* bedroom
(previous pages) is decorated with frescoes
by painter Fred Calmets, while Room 3 was designed
by the aKa collective, noted for their work in 3D
(don't forget your glasses!).

in Saint-Valery-sur-Somme

The lonely sea and the sky

Géraldine Senlis
LE SQUARE SEVEN
Guest rooms
7 rue de l'Echaux,
80230 Saint-Valery-sur-Somme
www.squareseven.com
+ 33 (0)6 70 90 41 73

Everyone comes back to Saint-Val.
On foot, by bike, on horseback, in the old
family Volvo, for a romantic weekend,
in hiking boots or barefoot. The Somme
estuary and the delightful village harbor
are rediscovered each time, like the first.
The seasons change, and the setting
is as charming and far away-from-it-all
as ever. Here are endless skies, the sea,
and the birds (everyone comes to the
Somme estuary to watch the birds).
But there are salt-marsh sheep, too,
and an old railway line, a beach shack
bar, even a population of seals.
Everyone finds their heart's content:
the seamen's chapel and cross,
the picturesque Courtgain quarter,
the Ville Haute. Géraldine has known
them all since childhood, and when
the opportunity arose to live here
all year round—umbrella and Wellington
boots at the ready—she didn't think
twice. Géraldine settled on a small house
in the old medieval town,
built of brick, gray stone, and black flint—
like the church wall next door.
The interior space was remodeled,
its walls stripped bare or given a new
treatment. Géraldine, a stylist by training,
has reinvented the decor, too, in her own
subtle, distinctive style.

Lines and volumes are simple, bordering
on the minimalist, like this trompe l'œil wall
concealing a doorway (facing page). Everywhere,
there are fine fabrics and subtle, discreet touches
of color: a bergère covered in crimson velvet,
vintage chairs, a 1950s bentwood armchair chair
covered in natural linen, a group of roses
standing tall in electric-blue glass bottles.

Géraldine has decorated the bedrooms in a sober,
understated but graphic style, attenuated by pale
colors and soft lines inspired by the ever-changing
hues of the broad horizons of the Somme estuary.

A secret patio garden

Annick Lestrohan
CASA HONORÉ
Guesthouse, decoration consultancy
123 rue Sainte, 13007 Marseille
www.casahonore.com
+ 33 (0)4 96 11 01 62

From the secret creeks of the calanques to the cosmopolitan crowds on the city's main thoroughfare, the Canébière, Marseille is France's most exotic mainland city, and the setting for Annick Lestrohan's adopted home: not Brazil, nor a Moroccan *riad*, but a little of each. Behind the imposing façade of the old Roux printworks, on a busy street of workshops above the Old Port, Annick—a professional designer with a string of credits to her name—has created a chic, off-beat townhouse centered on an exceptional patio garden. The industrial building offers some four thousand square feet: enough space for expansive self-expression, whatever its actual size. On the ground floor, a series of interconnecting rooms are the backdrop to an urban lifestyle adapted to the changing seasons: the huge ornamental pond is the focal point of a walkway planted with palm trees, serving an array of salons furnished with deep sofas. Annick has five children already, and now a sixth—Honoré, the name she has chosen for her wide-ranging lifestyle business: a fashion collection, restaurant, and decoration consultancy. Most importantly, though, Casa Honoré is her home.

Honoré includes a collection of fine linens, furniture, and lighting, and an expert decoration service. The open-work walls resemble traditional *moucharabieh* screens; original lamps in straw, wicker, or an industrial style set the tone for each room. Honoré offers a distinctive mix of industrial, Danish, rustic, Moroccan, and vintage styles and influences: a heady flavor of faraway places.

Far Horizons

A beachside cabin, a flowery deck,
a pontoon-like terrace: irresistible
invitations to step aboard.

In the shade of the pines

Nicole and William Joinau
LA MAISON DU BASSIN
Hotel, bistro
5 rue des Pionniers, 33950 Lège-Cap-Ferret
www.lamaisondubassin.com
+ 33 (0)5 56 60 60 63

Fifteen years ago, Nicole and William Joinau took a gamble that paid off—realizing their wild dream of converting an old hotel, on a whim and a prayer. The building proved a sound starting point: completed in 1899, it has been adopted by successive generations of vacationers on the Cap Ferret peninsula. When the Joinaus took over, they dedicated themselves to creating a stylish travelers' retreat, a veritable home-from-home. Soon, the blue-painted wooden verandah was entwined with wisteria. The interior, refurbished and decorated with flea-market finds and thoughtful extra touches over the years, is suffused with the timeless style of a much-loved family seaside retreat. The guest rooms, terrace, bistro, and bar offer a delightfully intimate, friendly atmosphere, and the hotel is a favorite venue for friends playing pétanque or for couples—from Paris to New York—holding romantic wedding ceremonies. The ultimate seal of approval.

Echoing the beach huts and chalets of Cap Ferret, wood is an essential feature
at the Maison du Bassin—untreated, varnished, painted, tinted, or lime washed,
it characterizes every corner of this atmospheric building. An old-fashioned
calendar hangs in the entrance hall. Vintage tennis rackets in faded cotton covers
and wooden frames stand as if waiting for a game.

From the wooden doors to the seascapes hanging on the walls, much of the furniture
and decor comes from L'Esprit du Cap, an antiques and bric-a-brac emporium run
by the Joinaus' neighbor and friend—a treasured source of new objects, from a collection
of nautical pennants to a painting of a storm at sea. Each of the hotel's eleven rooms
is unique and individually decorated, to the delight of its regular guests.

Bathing beauties

Françoise and Mathieu Lesné-Pradet
LE CLOS JOSÉPHINE
Guesthouse
8 rue de la Ville Assier, 35800 Saint-Briac-sur-Mer
www.02-chambre-hote-charme-briac.com
+ 33 (0)2 99 88 38 42

Vacations at Saint-Briac follow a timeless ritual. During the Belle Époque, travelers visiting the Côte d'Emeraude to bathe in the briny would gather on their first evening for dinner at the Auberge de la Croix Rouge. Now, the same building has been transformed by Françoise and her son Mathieu into a colorful, stylish guesthouse. After a full year of building work and refurbishment, the interior of this typical Breton inn has been completely remodeled and redecorated, bringing a touch of classic New England style to the north coast of Brittany. At the back of the house, in place of the old dining room, a huge verandah opens onto the garden and pool, gleaming with emerald light—a tempting alternative to the region's sweeping beaches. As a gentle reminder, each room is named after one of the ten within reach of this delightful seaside resort, including Grande and Petite Salinette, Le Bechet, La Garde, and Le Port Hue.

The walls are covered with whitewashed wainscoting dotted
with vintage paintings and family portraits, evoking the golden age of France's
merchant navy, and voyages to far-flung lands. Voyages that have inspired
Françoise's distinctive style, incorporating flea-market finds like ships' gangway doors,
model boats, or a small Louis Vuitton suitcase.

Deckchair stripes, for a breath of sea air

As a counterpoint to the level horizon traced by the paneling and bedheads,
the house's chairs and armchairs are covered with deckchair-striped fabrics
in colors redolent of the coastal landscapes of Brittany.

Vintage sheets, fine linen and embroidery,
evanescent curtains, loose covers,
and cashmere throws: Le Clos Joséphine
is a haven of cocooning.

For a garden, the sea

Marie-Claude and Alain Pelé
UNE CHAMBRE D'HÔTES À DAHOUËT
Guesthouse
11 chemin du Bignon, 22370 Pléneuf-Val-André
unechambredhotes.canalblog.com
+ 33 (0)2 96 72 88 93

A private house, sheltered (say the locals) by the fabled micro-climate of the Baie de Saint-Brieuc, on Brittany's north coast. A place for family vacations, where generations meet for the long summer break. Sailing school, rock-pooling for shellfish, catching lobsters in pots, tennis tournaments, a round of golf, hikes along the coastal path (the Sentier des Douaniers), high tides, and crumbling sandcastles. Marie-Claude and Alain have created the perfect family vacation house, and their own seaside home. With its clapboard façade and English-style bay and sash windows, wooden verandah, and balconies inspired by the architecture of the region's grand seaside villas, the building is flooded with natural light. The broad terrace, sheltered from the prevailing wind (and prying eyes), is a relaxing haven in all weathers. A place where guests are content to while away the hours, dreaming that maybe one day they could live nearby.

The huge bookcases were made to measure
by a joiner friend, for alcoves either side
of the chimney piece (a flea-market find).
A leather club armchair and Lloyd Loom chairs offer
their owner, Alain, a well-deserved chance
to relax—he built the house himself, from scratch.

On a background of shifting gray, arranged
on a stylish chest of drawers, seashells
and a dressmaker's dummy keep company
with a vase. With an antique globe underneath,
a nineteenth-century dressing table, accompanied
by flowers and a mannequin, confers on this room
a romantic atmosphere.

Shells, majolica, and *petit blanc* figurines

Stormy gray, wine-dark purple, pale blue-gray, or turquoise. As a counterpoint to the immaculate
white finish of traditional *petit blanc* figurines from the Quimper earthenware factory, Marie-Claude Pelé
gives free rein to her love of color, with an ebullient palette extending out into the garden.
Planted with roses, agapanthus, palm trees, and seaside flora, the abundant flower beds encapsulate
the house's serene sense of well-being, close to the living garden of the sea.

Chalets and seashells

Jane and Olivier Roellinger
LES GÎTES MARINS DES MAISONS DE BRICOURT
Cottages
62 rue des Rimains, 35260 Cancale
www.maisons-de-bricourt.com
+ 33 (0)2 99 89 64 76

The coastal path winds along the broad foreshore, heady with the fragrance of pine trees, privet, and gorse. The walker stops to admire the stunning ancient "rock of marvels"—Mont Saint-Michel—then, catching his breath and continuing on his way, revels in the mingled seascapes and skies of the bay. Olivier Roellinger loves accompanying visitors along the path from his hotel and restaurant at Château Richeux to the Pointe du Grouin. Overlooking the offshore islet known as the Rocher de Cancale, in the grounds of the Roellingers' cottage hotel, Les Rimains, Olivier's wife Jane has installed a collection of family vacation cottages: Berniques, Bigorneau, Crevette, Olivette, and Touline. The delightful "cabins" are surrounded by trees and abundant greenery, each opening onto the gardens and the maritime vegetable plot sloping gently down to the sea. Guests are free to gather herbs and seasonal vegetables here, to cook for themselves, or to dine at the Château Richeux table, where they can enjoy spiced sweetmeats under the watchful eye of the resident chef and his accomplished team.

Children love the cleverly redesigned berth beds;
their parents appreciate the refined decor.

A fourth house has recently joined
the fleet, architect-designed,
with striking contemporary lines.

A long, quiet voyage

Nathalie and Patrick Hubier
LE VAL DE BRANGON
Guesthouse
Lieu-dit Brangon, 56870 Baden
www.levaldebrangon.com
+ 33 (0)2 97 57 06 05

Partir au hasard. Travel by chance: the phrase invites visitors to explore Le Val de Brangon—Nathalie and Patrick Hubier's guesthouse—online, and in real life. The house is a vast, traditional *longère,* some 120 feet from end to end, nestling between the seaway and lush countryside of the Gulf of Morbihan, in southeastern Brittany. Built in 1824 on the estate of the Château de Kergonano, between the Auray River and the town of Larmor Baden, the former farmhouse was big enough to provide a home for the Hubiers' extensive collections (the couple are dedicated antiquers and travelers). Treasures caught in their net over the years include chunks of ironwork, a ship's porthole, a cargo-ship funnel, wooden doors from India, a propeller, a model plane, stylish furniture, and a host of everyday objects. Scrubbed up, recycled, and put to new uses—practical or purely decorative—everything has found its proper place in the generously proportioned, rambling house that stands waiting to be explored, like a detour on a well-trodden trail of antique shops, skipping from one delightful, unexpected find to the next.

Complementing the *longère*'s original stone chimney
and walls, the owners have added a touch of bold
industrial chic, with untreated metal fittings
and distressed wood—as seen here in the kitchen,
by the design workshop *De bouche à oreille*.

Recette :
Pâte à crêpes
Temps de préparation 1h45
Pour 12 personnes.

Ingrédients
· 3 oeufs
· 250 g de lait écrémé
· 30 g de beurre allégé
· 125 g de farine T55
· 9.5 g de sel
· 5 g d'huile arachide
· 50 g de rhum

- Tamiser la farine dans un grand saladier pour éviter d'obtenir des grumeaux.
- Faire fondre le beurre.
- Mélanger délicatement dans le saladier les oeufs, le lait, le beurre, la farine, le sel, le rhum.
- Battre au mixeur ou au fouet pendant une minute.

Upstairs, the bedrooms lead off a long passageway
under the eaves, each named in honor of Nathalie
and Patrick's passion for their home region,
and faraway places alike. Unsurprisingly,
perhaps, the couple collects vintage captains'
trunks—ready to set sail!

The *longère*'s walls are clad in rusted corrugated iron, coated in traditional red plaster, or stripped back to their original, centuries-old granite. The result is a simple, authentic look mixing rustic, industrial, and sea-port influences.

In the entrance, a cargo-ship's funnel stands like a sculpture against the bare
stone wall, in striking counterpoint to the lush, green landscape to the rear
of the house, overlooking a twelve-acre walnut orchard, beyond which lie
the tranquil waters of the Gulf of Morbihan.

Island Life

On a peninsula, across a causeway,
a short ferry-ride away: an island dream
house, to share or keep all to yourself.

Until the weather lifts

Sophie Véron
LE MANOIR DE COUTAINVILLE
Guesthouse and restaurant
2 rue de la Maugerie, 50230 Agon-Coutainville
www.manoir-de-coutainville.com
+ 33 (0)2 33 47 05 90

Sophie adores the peninsula for its sweeping beaches, the lunar atmosphere of the dunes, and the seascapes and countryside with their ever-changing light and weather. Gazing out over the tousled vegetation of the Cotentin, and across the sea to the Channel Islands, her manor house in the old quarter of Coutainville was the setting for Sophie's childhood family vacations. Today, her warm hospitality is fueled by happy memories of good times with friends and family, and huge, celebratory meals. In the middle of an open field surrounded by high granite walls, the old estate (dating back to the fifteenth century) includes the manor house, a pigeon loft, the seneschal's house, and a barn, all decorated in authentic style, with heirloom furniture, eclectic collections of candlesticks and earthenware, beach games, and wicker baskets. Throw in a trayful of Blainville oysters, Granville shellfish, wild herbs and vegetables fresh from the sandy, salty soil, add a generous dash of good humor from the mistress of the house, and you have the perfect recipe for an island vacation, cut off from the world until the weather lifts.

The manor's outbuildings have been transformed
into a delightful small guesthouse. Next to the fire
stands a wing armchair covered in rich leather
and decked with a tartan throw, complementing
a palette of textiles including finely striped mattress
ticking. The huge kitchen is a delight to share
in all seasons.

Each bedroom is an intimate haven, to (re)discover on your return
from the beach—individually furnished in Gustavian or rococo style,
with a mix of sophisticated and rustic materials (everything from raw concrete
to wicker), and a scattering of chic and ethnic decorative objects.
The Sénéchal features gray-painted walls, bric-a-brac furniture, and a Japanese
zinc bathtub facing the bed—for a touch of manorial Zen.

A traditional family hotel

Delphine and Mathieu Dubos
L'HÔTEL DES DEUX MERS
Family hotel
8 avenue Surcouf, Penthièvre Plage 56510,
Saint Pierre Quiberon
hotel-des-deux-mers.com
+ 33 (0)2 97 52 33 75

Belle-Île floats on the horizon, and the Quiberon peninsula stretches out from the mainland to the very last landing stage, like an invitation to set sail, a foretaste of the bracing ocean air. Bordering the Côte Sauvage—the peninsula's celebrated, wild Atlantic coastline of spectacular cliffs and expansive beaches—the Hôtel des Deux Mers is a fine old hotel, built in the 1930s, in the heyday of the family seaside vacation. High ceilings, polished hardwood floors, a huge verandah, and a garden that reaches down to the beach—the Deux Mers has it all. Delphine and Mathieu Dubos fell in love with the building—and its setting—at first sight, bought it with little thought for the gargantuan task ahead, and dedicated themselves to bringing the place up to date. Bedrooms were extended to become family suites, floors were covered with sisal matting, dark wooden paneling was repainted in soft gray. The hotel's services were given a makeover, too, with a host of ideas for families from their very first season: picnic baskets on request, bicycles available to all guests, even a flotilla of sand yachts—the perfect way to enjoy the windswept beach nearby.

The huge communal dining room—the setting
for breakfast and afternoon tea—opens
onto the verandah at the rear of the hotel.
Adirondack chairs and benches piled
with thick cushions are the perfect setting
for vacation reading or a game of chess.

Simple furniture and antique-shop finds recreate the atmosphere
of a much-loved family vacation home. The guest rooms are furnished
with wicker armchairs, *bonnetières,* and cupboards patinated by a friend and
bric-a-brac dealer from La Trinité-sur-Mer. Rooms and communal spaces
are decorated in a palette of soft grays with subtle touches of color.

Walking in the dunes, feeling the wind in your hair, breathing the salty sea air,
flying a kite. After a trip to the beach, each hotel room
is a welcoming cocoon, a place to read or sit on the balcony,
watching the sun dip below the ocean horizon.

Timeless charm

Catherine and Alain Brunel
LA MAISON DOUCE
Hotel
25 rue Mérindot, 17410 Saint-Martin-de-Ré
www.lamaisondouce.com
+ 33 (0)5 46 09 20 20

Time out. The news of the day can wait....
Here, all that matters is an enchanting
island home, a retreat from the world
beyond. Catherine and Alain dropped
everything to come and live here,
acquiring the house ten years ago
and changing very little since then—just
enough to make the most of what was
already there. Trips to the attic produced
aged floorboards, an outsize wooden
cupboard. The soul of the house laid bare.
Visitors to the island village of Saint-Martin-
de-Ré, midway along France's Atlantic
seaboard, discover La Maison Douce
with delight, in the maze of streets
that make up its historic quarter.
Dating from the eighteenth and
nineteenth centuries, the building
comprises a guesthouse and the owners'
home, both opening onto a romantic
garden—the setting for lazy afternoon
teas in summer. Each guest room
is a cocoon of soft colors, filmy fabrics,
and heavy, luxurious linens. In the sitting
room, Catherine and Alain have chosen
rich colors for the walls (changing the
scheme when the mood takes them),
against which empty frames hang
dreaming of unseen pictures, beyond.

In the beginning, Catherine and Alain created a guesthouse, with a handful
of simply furnished bedrooms painted in shades of camel, ash gray, violet,
chocolate, and white. The decor plays on juxtapositions
of color and trompe l'oeil, finished with a fine fillet in a darker, contrasting shade.
Other rooms were renovated around the garden, and the house became
a hotel, losing none of its original, timeless charm.

LE PHARE DE RÉ

JOURNAL D'INTÉRÊT LOCAL, D'ANNONCES ET D'AVIS DIVERS

Cette semaine, notre supplément !

Bientôt sur les étals

In search of lost time

Florence and Roger Mouza
AU TEMPS RETROUVÉ
Guesthouse
30 rue du Havre, 17590 Ars-en-Ré
www.autempsretrouve.com
+ 33 (0)6 82 57 96 09

Tea with apple crêpes, and rich cakes of chestnut, raspberry, and agar. All year round, Florence serves delicious brunches and afternoon teas in her elegant house at the tip of the Ile de Ré—a soothing haven of hospitality, dedicated to recapturing the slower pace of a bygone age. A place of Proustian atmosphere and attention to detail, both carefully choreographed and delightfully spontaneous. A former dancer and a seasoned traveler from India to Morocco, Florence has dropped anchor in the island village of Ars-en-Ré, renovating her home using simple, natural materials: recycled pine floorboards line the walls, insulated with lime wash and hemp, while the floors are covered with traditional cement tiles by Agnès Emery. Furniture and everyday objects are picked up at bric-a-brac and antiques markets, for fun, old-fashioned comfort, and that indefinable feel-good factor.

Tanned leather, hemp, linen,
and fine embroidery

 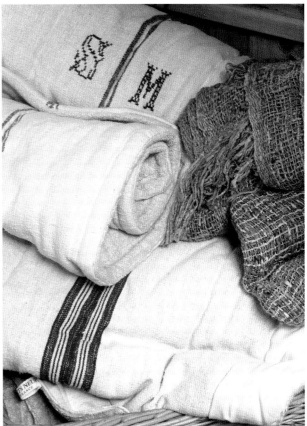

Canvas, woven hemp bags, and plump, finely embroidered cushions are piled on beds
and sofas. Found objects—from a collection of dried starfish to a slip-cast tea service, glass cloches,
a tinkling chandelier, and a simple pair of vintage slippers—are dotted from room to room, creating
a delightful, harmonious atmosphere, lulled by a soundtrack of retro jazz courtesy of Chet Baker.

A diaphanous veil floats on the frame
of a four-poster bed, against a backdrop of natural,
chalk-textured colors. In the neighboring bedroom,
the bathroom is open to the wider space,
offset by a dark, muted purple.

Seaside Souvenirs

Touching or forgotten, bric-a-brac
or collectors' pieces—a wealth of
decorative objects reflect our endless
desire to live by and with the sea.

A cabinet of curiosities

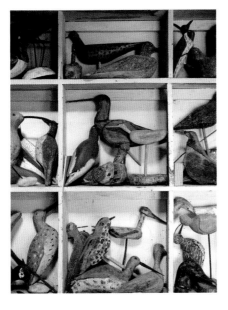

Sophie and Patrick Deloison
ANTIQUITÉS DELOISON
Antiques
1 quai du Romerel, 80230 Saint-Valery-sur-Somme
www.picardieweb.com/deloison
+ 33 (0)3 22 26 92 17

There are still people who discover the Somme estuary like Christopher Columbus stepping ashore in the New World. This quiet estuary on the Channel coast of northern France is a fascinating world apart. Patrick Deloison was born here, and played as a child on the narrow streets of the old harbor. Today, with his wife Sophie, he's a mine of information on the finer points of local history, his delight undimmed at the endless ritual of the tides, the shifting light of the bay, its ever-changing moods. Patrick pursues his trade as an antiques dealer with the same passionate interest, collecting decoys of all kinds (ducks, curlews, owls, magpies—the Somme estuary is famous for its birdlife), dioramas, and folk art objects, fueling the evolving displays in the couple's private house and business headquarters, built by Sophie's grandfather in the 1950s. Sophie and Patrick have extended the original building, with a huge two-story wooden verandah overlooking the garden, finished in black weatherboarding, topped with a balcony deck, and lit by two large portholes cut into the side walls, like an elegant liner, ready to sail the seven seas.

The objects and decor in this unusual antique-
dealer's home change as new finds are acquired
or sold, ebbing and flowing with the seasons
and tides. Folk art objects are displayed alongside
tribal sculptures or an exotic, Orientalist terra-cotta
statuette. Like a cabinet of curiosities, amassed
by a seafaring explorer of old.

Where time stands still

Laure Chopy
LE DONJON
Antiques and bric-a-brac, cottage
43 rue Paul Besson, 14360 Trouville-sur-Mer
www.trouvillesurmer.org/LEDONJON
+ 33 (0)6 18 95 51 90

In search of paradise, some might dream of a Moorish castle in Spain. Antiques dealer and gourmet Laure Chopy found her ideal *castillo* in the Normandy town of Trouville: a townhouse formerly owned by a gentleman by the fitting name of Paradis. Le Donjon was built in the late nineteenth century, at the heart of Trouville's winding streets and flowery seafront. The tall white building echoes the Moorish style popular at the time, decked with balconies and terraces gazing out to the misty ocean horizon. Divided into separate dwellings, the building today houses Laure's unconventional antiques emporium, a vacation apartment, and her private home, occupying the grand reception rooms of the original villa, on the upper floor. Subtle, Gustavian colors offset French furnishings from Louis XV to the Empire period, dotted with displays of Laure's myriad collections of objects. Like a collector's cabinet of curiosities, shellfish and sea fans are displayed in a *globe de mariée* (a glass cloche once used to display a bride's wedding bouquet) and a bouquet of dried hydrangea blooms decorates a Medici vase, suffused by the soft, bohemian light of the Normandy coast.

In the bedroom and living room,
the owner's collections are displayed
on fine pieces of eighteenth-century painted
furniture bought in Italy. A pair of period figurines
stands conspiratorially close, as if holding a private
conference. A single starfish, placed beneath
a delicate glass dome, completes the scene.

The house at land's end

Paul Townsend
LA BROCANTE D'OUESSANT
Island bric-a-brac
Stan Ar Glan, Ouessant
+ 33 (0)2 98 48 87 87

An antiques and bric-a-brac shop, on Ouessant island, France's westernmost outpost. Paul Townsend (known locally as *l'anglais,* although his grandfather was a Ouessant fisherman) came ashore here twenty years ago in search of his family roots, and never left. An established antiques dealer, he continued to ply his trade on the island, reflecting its maritime heritage. Three times a year, a container arrives full of treasures collected on trips back to England—local antiques are scarce, although the island's tradition of beachcombing and recycling continues to flourish, harvesting fragments of old wrecks, sometimes even the cargoes of doomed container ships. Huddled together in hamlets along the island's few roads, Ouessant's picturesque cottages were traditionally constructed from wood collected on the storm-washed foreshore. The resulting partition screens and carved furniture were painted to mask the mismatched timber. Paul has left his island home untouched, as a natural setting for his collection of seafaring objects—some still sourced from locals and mariners, each piece telling the story of a simple life lived at the edge of the world.

Simple objects evoking the lives
and memories of seafaring folk

In a neighboring house, converted to a tearoom, Paul displays a life-sized half-hull from the harbor
in Lampaul, Ouessant's main town. Model boats, ship's lanterns, deck fittings, lifebelts,
and portholes—Paul's carefully sourced collection of maritime objects is a testimony to the lives
of seafaring folk. Other pieces speak of those left waiting ashore: minutely detailed dioramas,
witches' balls in metallized glass, touching ex-votos, and protective statues of the Virgin Mary
(the sailors' *bonne mère*), like those seen dotting the island's winding roads.

Beachcombing bric-a-brac

Dominique and Jean-Pierre
LA LANGOUSTE BLEUE
Bric-a-brac boutique
44 Grande Rue, 35800 Saint-Briac-sur-Mer

Dominique and Jean-Pierre's delicious, beachfront bric-a-brac business is a cheery assortment of treasures, packed with vintage textiles and nightshirts, ornaments, children's toys, and folk art. Their home is as picturesque as the shop, and Dominique presides here with characteristic delight. The small Breton stone house has been transformed into an exquisite seaside cottage, surrounded by a rambling, luxuriant garden to share with family and friends—a place for sunbathing, dining by candlelight, chatting quietly with friends, enjoying an afternoon nap. Children dart here and there, shouting, laughing, playing. Further away, in a quiet corner, Jean-Pierre's office and private retreat is installed in a beach-style chalet. Everyone has their favorite spot, in the house and garden alike. But everyone gathers at the appointed time, to savor lunch served by Dominique, picnic style or seated around the huge dining table, for the assembled crew.

The kitchen is decorated in a bright combination
of yellows and greens, inspired by points
south (Provence, Morocco) and the iconic
colors of Dominique's collection of Quimper
earthenware—one of her many passions.

Ships in bottles, boxes covered in shells, terra-cotta
figurines from L'Isle-Adam or Villenauxe-la-Grande,
works of folk art—Dominique adores picturesque
objects and naïf art inspired by the seafaring life.

In good company

Françoise and Michel Busson-Wagner
LA SEIGNEURIE
Guesthouse
35114 Saint-Benoît-des-Ondes
la-seigneurie-des-ondes.net
+ 33 (0)2 99 58 62 96

Just getting here is a joy in itself.
As the last stop on the traditional
pilgrimage to the bay of Mont Saint-
Michel, La Seigneurie stands serenely
behind high granite walls. Built in the
twelfth century, the original house
has been extended, transformed,
demolished, and reconstructed
over the centuries. The setting is a haven
of charm, and its history is fascinating,
too—Françoise and Michel have
breathed new life into the house,
inherited from a long line of corsairs
and shipbuilders from nearby Saint-Malo.
Far from submitting meekly
to the immutable heritage of its massive
stone walls, Françoise—a former antiques
dealer—has tackled it head-on,
with taste and flair, due respect
and an extra dose of tough love.
A passionate collector of eighteenth-
century decorative arts, she has thrown
herself into the task of creating
a comfortable, contemporary,
ephemeral interior. The woodwork
and walls (inside and out) are often
repainted with fresh colors; and
a new bedroom is opening soon,
in the gardener's annex.

Scallop shells, the traditional gift of thanks left
by pilgrims on the route to Santiago de Compostela,
are pressed into the walls or displayed here,
on a delicate wire support. Françoise and Michel
take a playful approach to decoration, finding new
uses for old objects, like the kitchen table, mounted
on the base of an old church pulpit.

Saffron yellow, terra-cotta red, faded blue: Françoise experiments
with her Farrow and Ball paints, mixing new shades of her own for the Seigneurie's
woodwork, inside and out. In the bedrooms, an old panettone box, compressed
cardboard suitcases, lengths of vintage linen hung like bridal veils,
and embroidered, monogrammed sheets add to the hotel's gentle charm.

In the Grande Cour suite, the alcove bed nestles beneath a mezzanine lined
with recycled wood paneling from a local church. Françoise accommodates solid
pieces of nineteenth- and twentieth-century furniture, placing an Imperial bench
alongside a pair of elegant, upright metal chairs brought back from the States—like
timeless treasures displayed on a traveler's return from a round-the-world voyage.

Log Book

Atlantic coast

AU TEMPS RETROUVÉ p. 156
Guesthouse
30 rue du Havre, 17590 Ars-en-Ré
www.autempsretrouve.com
+ 33 (0)6 82 57 69 09

LA MAISON DU BASSIN p. 82
Hotel, bistro
5 rue des Pionniers, 33950 Lège-Cap-Ferret
www.lamaisondubassin.com
+ 33 (0)5 56 60 60 63

LA MAISON DOUCE p. 148
Hotel
25 rue Mérindot, 17410 Saint-Martin-de-Ré
www.lamaisondouce.com
+ 33 (0)5 46 09 20 20

LE SÉNÉCHAL p. 18
Hotel and guesthouses
6 rue Gambetta, 17590 Ars-en-Ré
www.hotel-le-senechal.com
+ 33 (0)5 46 29 40 42

Brittany

LA BROCANTE D'OUESSANT p. 180
Island bric-a-brac
Stang Ar Glan, Ouessant
+ 33 (0)2 98 48 87 87

UNE CHAMBRE D'HÔTES À DAHOUËT p. 98
Guesthouse
11 chemin du Bignon, 22370 Pléneuf-Val-André
unechambredhotes.canalblog.com
+ 33 (0)2 96 72 88 93

LE CLOS JOSÉPHINE p. 88
Guesthouse
8 rue de la Ville Assier, 35800 Saint-Briac-sur-Mer
www.02-chambre-hote-charme-briac.com
+ 33 (0)2 99 88 38 42

LES GÎTES MARINS DES MAISONS DE BRICOURT
p. 106
Cottages
62 rue des Rimains, 35260 Cancale
www.maisons-de-bricourt.com
+ 33 (0)2 99 89 64 76

L'HÔTEL DES DEUX MERS p. 138
Family hotel
8 avenue Surcouf, Penthièvre Plage 56510,
Saint Pierre Quiberon
hotel-des-deux-mers.com
+ 33 (0)2 97 52 33 75

KERELEVEN p. 46
Guesthouse
11 chemin de la Hune, 56470 La Trinité-sur-Mer
www.kereleven.com
+ 33 (0)2 97 55 75 07

LA LANGOUSTE BLEUE p. 186
Bric-a-brac boutique
44 Grande Rue, 35800 Saint-Briac-sur-Mer

LA SEIGNEURIE p. 194
Guesthouse
35114 Saint-Benoît-des-Ondes
la-seigneurie-des-ondes.net
+ 33 (0)2 99 58 62 96

LE VAL DE BRANGON p. 116
Guesthouse
Lieu-dit Brangon, 56870 Baden
www.levaldebrangon.com
+ 33 (0)2 97 57 06 05

Normandy

LE DONJON p. 172
Antiques and bric-a-brac, cottage
43 rue Paul Besson, 14360 Trouville-sur-Mer
www.trouvillesurmer.org/LEDONJON
+ 33 (0)6 18 95 51 90

LE MANOIR DE COUTAINVILLE p. 128
Guesthouse and restaurant
2 rue de la Maugerie, 50230 Agon-Coutainville
www.manoir-de-coutainville.com
+ 33 (0)2 33 47 05 90

Picardy

ANTIQUITES DELOISON p. 166
1 quai du Romerel, 80230 Saint-Valery-sur-Somme
www.picardieweb.com/deloison
+ 33 (0)3 22 26 92 17

LE LOFT p. 10
Vacation apartment
1 quai du Romerel, 80230 Saint-Valery-sur-Somme
www.picardieweb.com/deloison
+ 33 (0)3 22 26 92 17

LE SQUARE SEVEN p. 64
Guest rooms
7 rue de l'Echaux, 80230 Saint-Valery-sur-Somme
www.squareseven.com
+ 33 (0)6 70 90 41 73

Provence
and the Côte d'Azur

AU VIEUX PANIER p. 56
Guesthouse
13 rue du Vieux Panier, 13002 Marseille
www.auvieuxpanier.com
+ 33 (0)4 91 91 23 72

CASA HONORÉ p. 74
Guesthouse, decoration consultancy
123 rue Sainte, 13007 Marseille
www.casahonore.com
+ 33 (0)4 96 11 01 62

LE CHÂTEAU DE SABLE p. 28
Guesthouse
Avenue des Anthémis, 83240 Cavalaire-sur-Mer
www.chateaudesable.net
+ 33 (0)4 94 00 45 90

LA MAISON DE CONSTANCE p. 34
Guesthouse
Hameau du Dattier, 83240 Cavalaire-sur-Mer
+ 33 (0)4 94 00 45 90

Acknowledgements

To everyone who opened the doors
of their seaside homes and lives.
To Farrow & Ball for their Tented Stripe
wallpaper, featured
on the title pages of each chapter.
To the team at Flammarion.
To the editorial team
at *Maisons Côté Ouest* magazine.
To the regional and departmental
tourist offices who made me so
welcome, especially Sylvie Blin,
Sophie Bougeard, Anne Dessery,
Sabine Canonica, Marie-Yvonne
Holley, Armelle Jouan, Christine
Kervadec, Armelle Le Goff, Valérie
Toche, and Lorene de Jessey.

Aquitaine, www.tourisme-aquitaine.fr
Brittany, www.brittanytourism.com
Bouches-du-Rhône, www.visitprovence.com
Calvados,
  www.calvados-tourisme.com
Charente-Maritime,
  www.en-charente-maritime.com
Finistère, www.finisteretourisme.com
Morbihan, www.morbihan.com
Provence, the Alps, and the Côte
  d'Azur, www.decouverte-paca.fr
Picardy, www.picardietourisme.com
Somme, www.somme-tourisme.com

To all my family, friends,
fellow sea lovers, travelers,
and antiquarians,
for their kind cooperation.
To Joseph and Lucien,
and to Laure, once again,
for the journeys to come.

Conception and Design: Sébastien Siraudeau
Blog: inmyvolvocar.blogspot.com
Translated from the French by Louise Rogers Lalaurie
Copyediting: Helen Woodhall
Typesetting: Claude-Olivier Four
Proofreading: Chrisoula Petridis
Color Separation: IGS, L'isle d'Espagnac, France
Printed in Italy by Canale

Simultaneously published in French as *Vivre à la Mer*
© Flammarion, SA, Paris, 2011

English-language edition
© Flammarion, SA, 2011
87, quai Panhard et Levassor
75647 Paris Cedex 13
editions.flammarion.com
11 12 13 3 2 1
ISBN: 978-2-08-020077-8
Dépôt légal: 04/2011